Drums
Rock Songbook

INTRODUCTION

Welcome to FastTrack™!

Hope you are ready to play some hits. Have you and your friends formed a band? Or do you feel like jamming with the CD? Either way, make sure you're relaxed and comfortable… it's time to play!

As always, don't try to bite off more than you can chew. If your arms are tired, take some time off. If you get frustrated, put down your sticks, sit back and just listen to the CD. If you forget a technique or rhythm, go back and learn it. If you're doing fine, think about finding an agent.

CONTENTS

ABOUT THE CD

Each song in the book is included on the CD, so you can hear how it sounds and play along when you're ready.

Each example on the CD is preceded by one measure of "clicks" to indicate the tempo and meter. Pan right to hear the drum part emphasized. Pan left to hear the accompaniment emphasized.

ISBN 978-1-4234-9574-1

CORPORATION
7777 W. BLUEMOUND RD. P.O. BOX 13819 MILWAUKEE, WI 53213

Visit Hal Leonard Online at
www.HalLeonard.com

LEARN SOMETHING NEW EACH DAY

We know you're eager to play, but first we need to explain a few new things. We'll make it brief—only one page...

Melody and Lyrics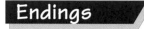

The additional musical staff on top shows you the song's melody and lyrics. This way, you can follow along more easily as you play your accompaniment part, whether you're playing, resting or showing off with a solo... well, sometimes drummers do get a solo.

And if you happen to be playing with a singer, this staff is their part.

Endings

1st and 2nd Endings

These are indicated by brackets and numbers:

Simply play the song through to the first ending, then repeat back to the first repeat sign, or beginning of the song (whichever is the case).

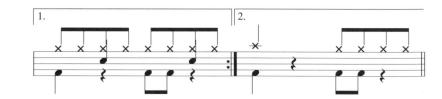

Play through the song again, but skip the first ending and play the second ending.

D.S. al Coda

When you see these words, go back and repeat from this symbol: 𝄋

Play until you see the words "To Coda" then skip to the Coda, indicated by this symbol: ⊕

Now just finish the song.

That's about it! Enjoy the music...

◆ ① Are You Gonna Be My Girl

Words and Music by Cameron Muncey and Nicholas Cester

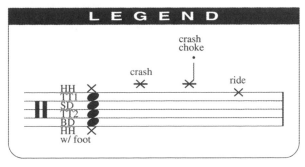

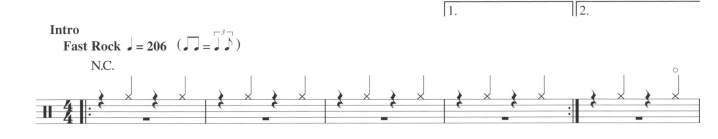

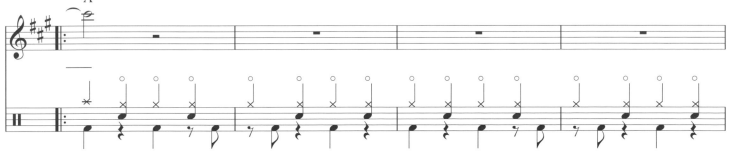

Verse

one, two, three, take my hand and come with me be - cause you look so fine and I

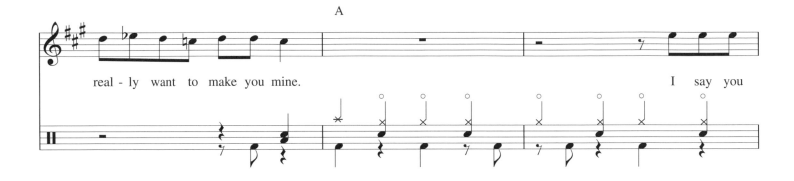

real - ly want to make you mine. I say you

look so fine and I real - ly want to make you mine.

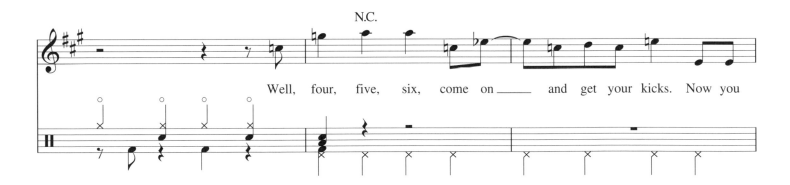

Well, four, five, six, come on _____ and get your kicks. Now you

don't need mon - ey { when you look like that, do you, hon - ey?
{ with a face like that, do ya?

Pre-Chorus

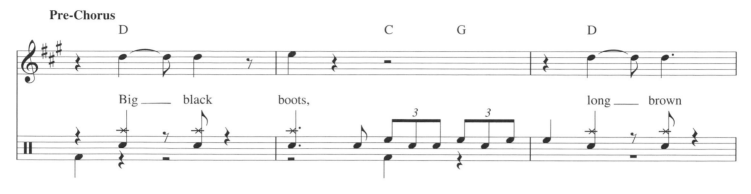

Big _____ black _____ boots, _____ long _____ brown

hair. _____ She's _____ so _____ sweet with _____ her

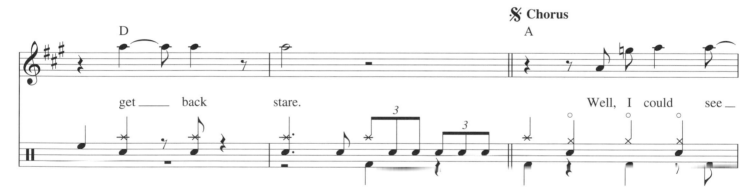

get _____ back _____ stare. _____ Well, I could see _____

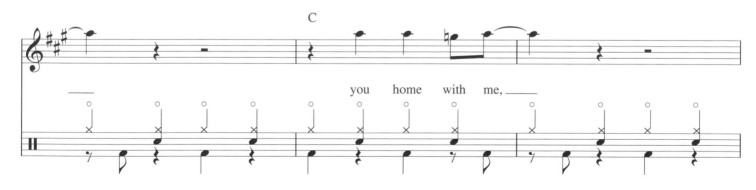

_____ you home with me, _____

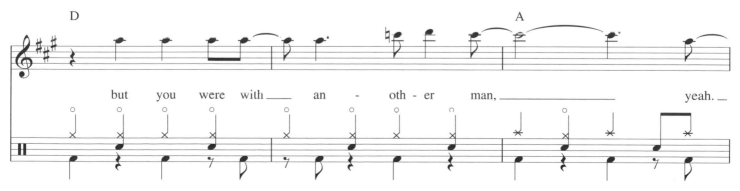

but you were with _____ an - oth - er man, _____ yeah. _____

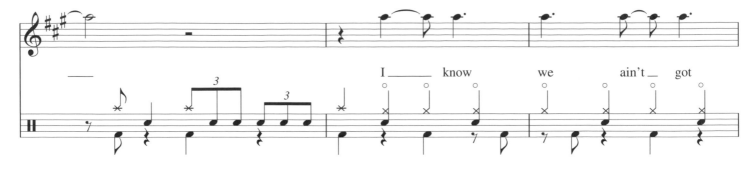

I _____ know we ain't ___ got

C   D

much to say ___   be - fore I let ___

To Coda ⊕

A

___ you get a - way, _____ yeah. ___

E   1.
                                                    G

N.C.   ⌐3⌐   ⌐3⌐

I said, "Are you gon - na be my girl?" ___

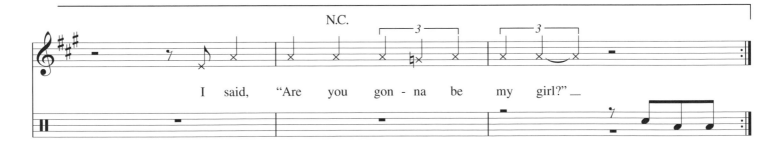

2. G   N.C.   ⌐3⌐   ⌐3⌐

I said, "Are you gon - na be my girl?"

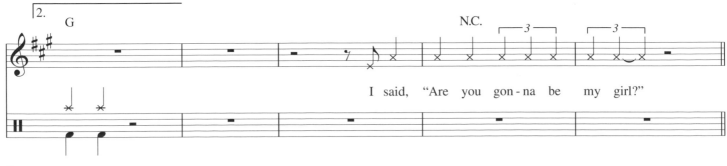

Interlude

D.S. al Coda

Ah. _____

⊕ Coda

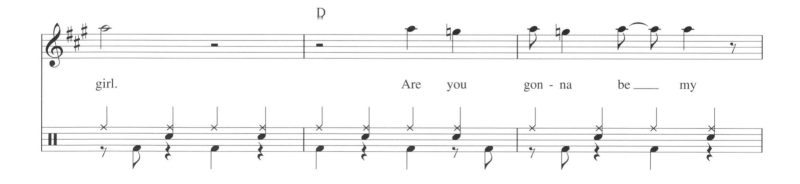

Uh, be my girl. ____   Be ____ my

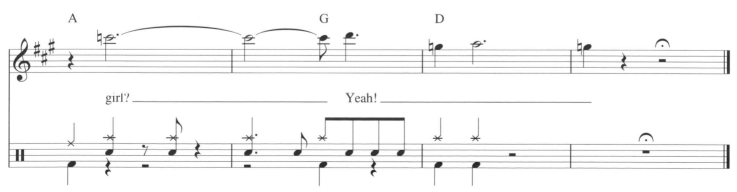

girl.   Are you gon - na be ____ my

girl? _____   Yeah! _____

◆② Clocks

Words and Music by Guy Berryman, Jon Buckland, Will Champion and Chris Martin

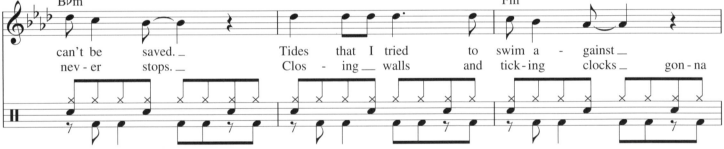

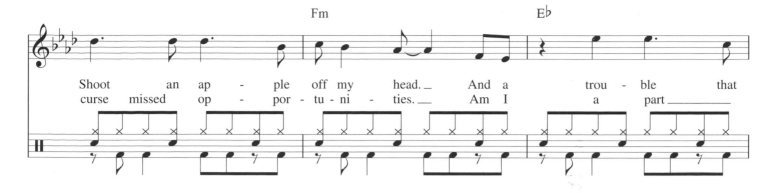

Shoot an ap - ple off my head. _ And a | trou - ble that
curse missed op - por - tu - ni - ties. _ Am I a part _____

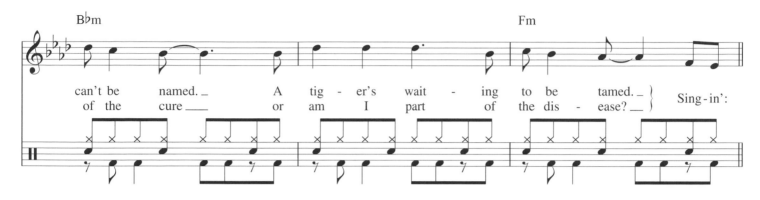

can't be named. _ A tig - er's wait - ing to be tamed. _ } Sing - in':
of the cure ___ or am I part of the dis - ease? _ }

Chorus

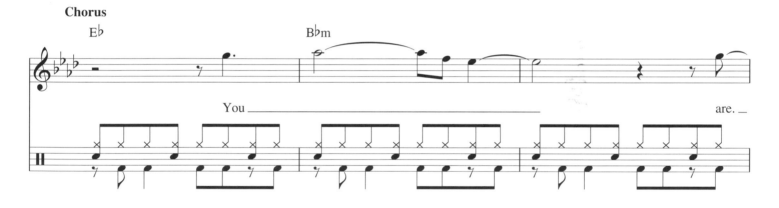

You _____ are. _

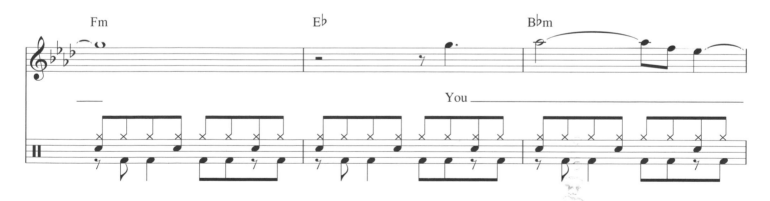

___ You _____

To Coda ⊕
Interlude

___ are. ___

⊕ Coda

You _____ are. __

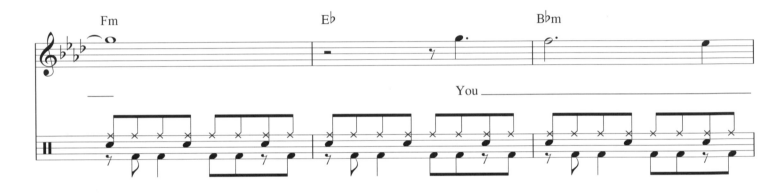

You _____

Bridge

are. __

⎧ 1., 3. And ⎫ noth-
⎨ 2. Oh, ⎬

⎧ 1., 2.

-ing else com - pares. _____

10

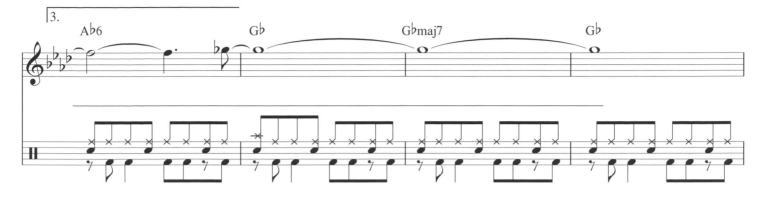

Breakdown

*Play 1st time only.

Interlude

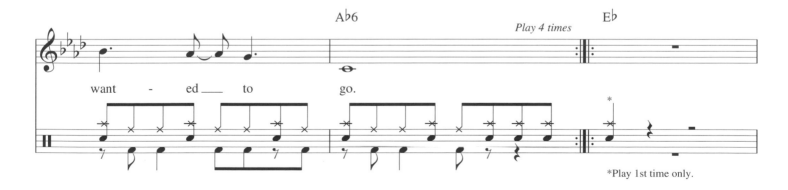

Outro

Home,   home, ___   where I

Play 4 times

want - ed ___ to   go.

*Play 1st time only.

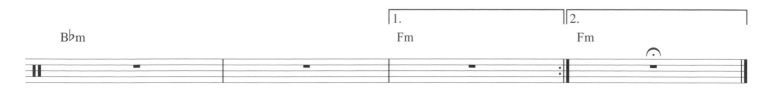

❸ Dani California

Words and Music by Anthony Kiedis, Flea, John Frusciante and Chad Smith

Intro
Moderately ♩ = 96

1. Get - ting born in the state of Mis - sis - sip - pi, Pa - pa was a cop - per and her ma - ma was a hip - pie.
2. Black ban - dan - a, __ sweet Lou - i - si - an - a, rob - bing on a bank __ in the state of In - di - an - a.
3. Push the fa - der, gift - ed an - i - mat - or, one __ for the now __ and e - lev - en for the lat - er.

In Al - a - bam - a, she __ would swing a ham - mer, price you got - ta pay __ when you break the pan - o - ram - a.
She's a run - ner, reb - el and a stun - ner, on her mer - ry way, __ say - ing, "Ba - by, what you gon - na?"
Nev - er made it up __ to Min - ne - so - ta, North Da - ko - ta man __ was a gun - ning for the quo - ta.

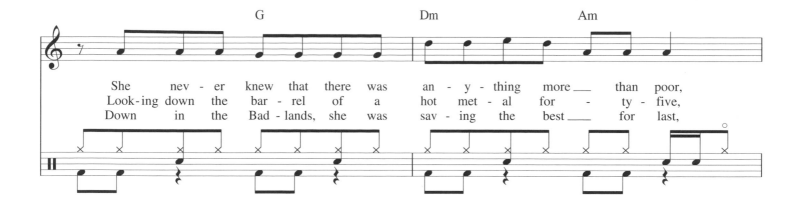

She nev-er knew that there was an-y-thing more ___ than poor,
Look-ing down the bar-rel of a hot met-al for-ty-five,
Down in the Bad-lands, she was sav-ing the best ___ for last,

1.

what in the world does your com-pa-ny take ___ me for?

2.

just an-oth-er way to sur-vive. ___
it on-ly hurts when I laugh. ___

Chorus

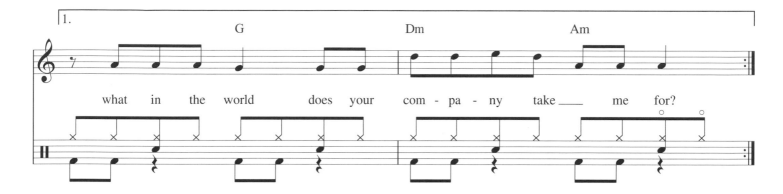

Cal - i - for - nia, rest ___ in peace. ___ Si - mul - ta -

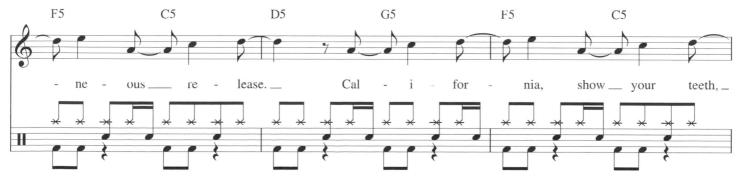

- ne - ous ___ re - lease. ___ Cal - i - for - nia, show ___ your teeth, ___

D5   G5   F5   C5   D5

she's my priest - ess, I'm your priest, yeah, yeah.

To Coda ⊕ **Bridge**

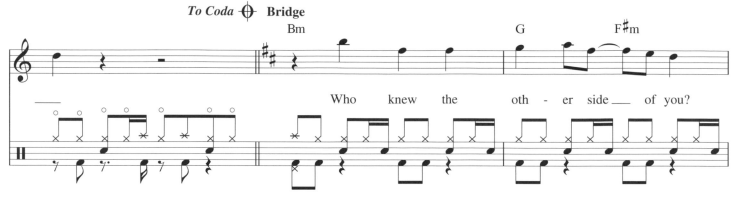

Bm   G   F#m

Who knew the oth - er side of you?

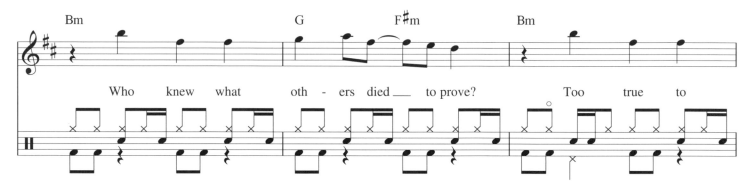

Bm   G   F#m   Bm

Who knew what oth - ers died to prove? Too true to

D.S. al Coda
(take 2nd ending)

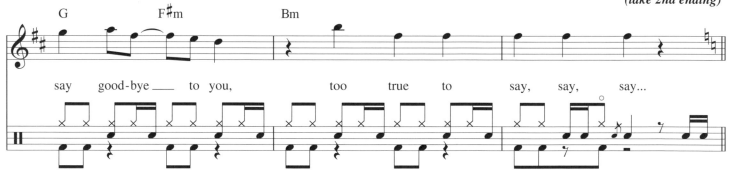

G   F#m   Bm

say good-bye to you, too true to say, say, say...

⊕ **Coda**
Outro

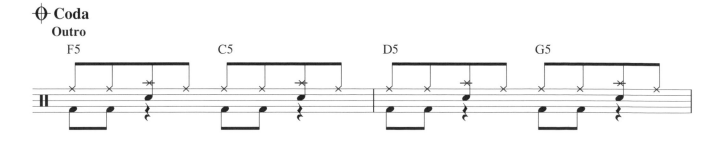

F5   C5   D5   G5

C5   D5

◆ Gives You Hell

Words and Music by Tyson Ritter and Nick Wheeler

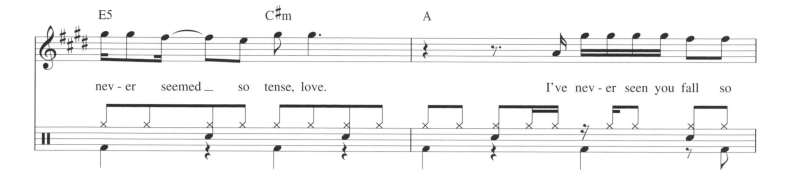

nev - er seemed __ so tense, love. I've nev - er seen you fall so

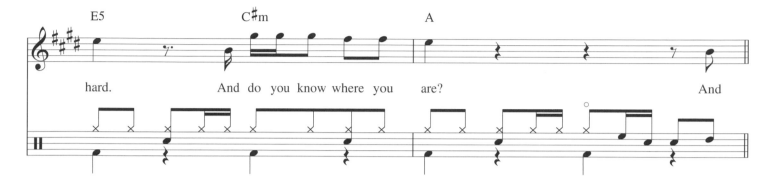

hard. And do you know where you are? And

Pre-Chorus

truth be told, __ I miss __ you. And truth be told, __ I'm ly -

𝄋 Chorus

ing. When you see my face, hope it gives you hell, hope it gives you

hell. When you walk my way, hope it gives you hell, hope it gives you __

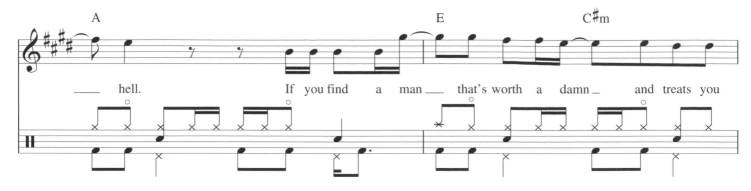

hell. If you find a man ___ that's worth a damn ___ and treats you

To Coda 1
To Coda 2

well, then he's a fool. ___ You're just as well, hope it gives you ___

Interlude

hell. I hope it gives ___ you hell.

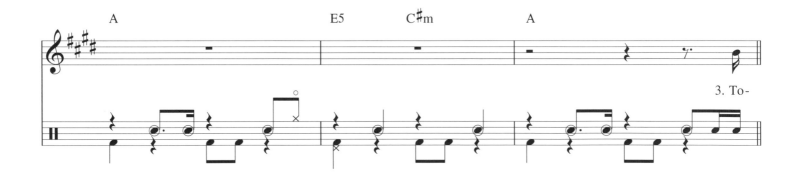

3. To-

Verse

mor-row you'll ___ be think - ing to ___ your - self, ___ yeah, where did it all ___ go ___

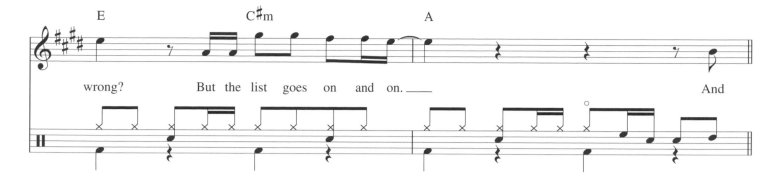

wrong? But the list goes on and on. ____ And

Pre-Chorus

truth be told, ____ I miss ____ you. And

D.S. al Coda 1

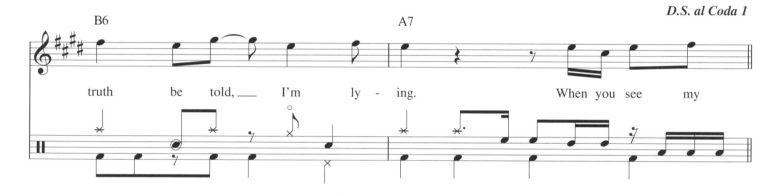

truth be told, ____ I'm ly - ing. When you see my

Coda 1

Bridge

____ hell. Now, you'll nev - er see ____ what

you've done ____ to me. ____ You can take back ____ your mem - o - ries, they're

no good to me. And here's to all your lies, you can

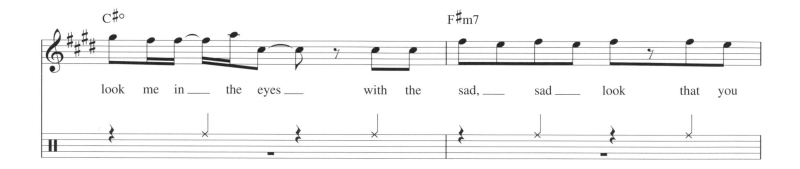

look me in the eyes with the sad, sad look that you

D.S. al Coda 2

wear so well. When you see my

Coda 2

Outro-Chorus

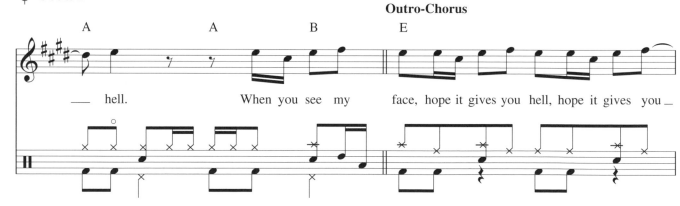

hell. When you see my face, hope it gives you hell, hope it gives you

hell. When you walk my way, hope it gives you hell, hope it gives you

hell. When you hear this song and you sing a - long, _ but you nev - er tell, _

_____ then you're the fool. I'm just as well, hope it gives you

song, I hope that it will give you

1.

hell. When you hear this

2.

hell. You can sing a -

long, I hope that it puts you through hell.

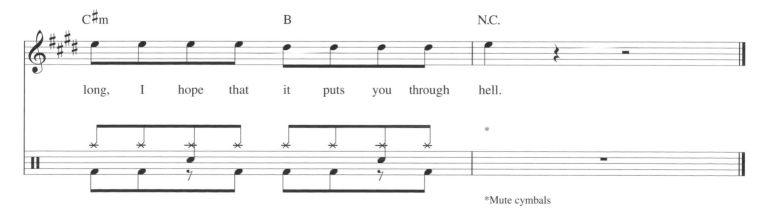

*Mute cymbals

◆ Grenade

**Words and Music by Bruno Mars, Ari Levine, Philip Lawrence,
Christopher Steven Brown, Claude Kelly and Andrew Wyatt**

Chorus

is, I'd catch a gre - nade ___ for ya, ___ throw my hand on a blade ___

___ for ya. ___ I'd jump in front of a train ___ for ya. ___

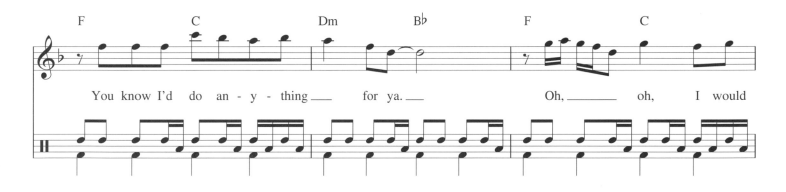

You know I'd do an - y - thing ___ for ya. ___ Oh, ___ oh, I would

go through all ___ this pain, ___ take a bul - let straight through my brain. ___

___ Yes, I would die ___ for you, ba - by, but you won't do the same.

Pre-Chorus

Oh, _____ oh, I would go through all ____ this pain, ____

take a bul - let straight through my brain. ____

To Coda ⊕

Yes, I would die ____ for you, ba - by,

Bridge

but you won't do the same. If my bod - y was on fi - re,

ooh, you'd watch me burn down in flames.

You said you loved me; you're a li - ar, 'cause you

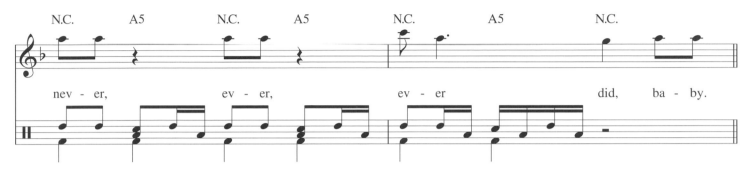

nev - er, ev - er, ev - er did, ba - by.

D.S. al Coda

Interlude

But dar - ling, I'd still catch a gre - nade

Coda

Outro

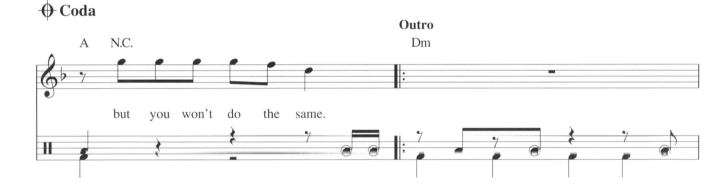

but you won't do the same.

{ No, you won't } do the same.
{ You nev - er }

1.
You would-n't do the same. No, no, no.
2.

Home

Words and Music by Chris Daughtry

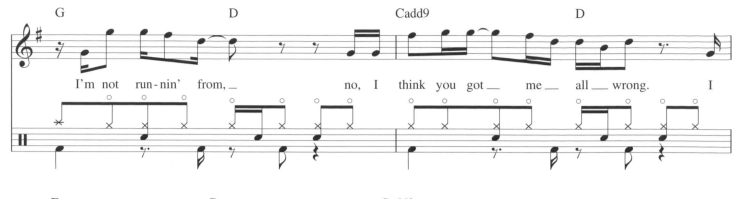

I'm not run-nin' from, __ no, I think you got __ me __ all __ wrong. I

don't re - gret __ this life I chose __ for me. __ But these

1.

To Coda ⊕

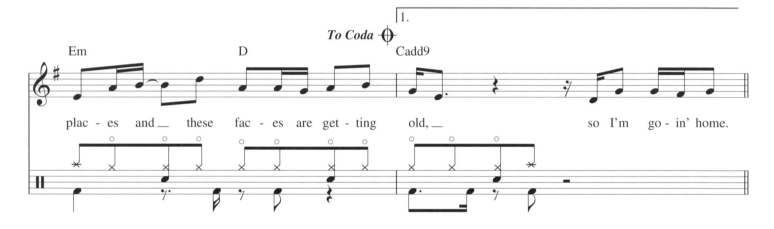

plac - es and __ these fac - es are get - ting old, __ so I'm go - in' home.

Interlude

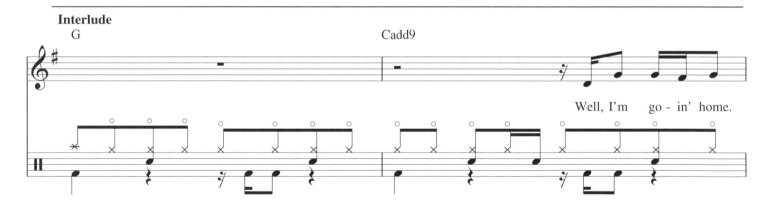

Well, I'm go - in' home.

2.

old. __

Bridge

Be care-ful what __ you wish for __ 'cause you just might get it all. __

__ You just might get it all _____ and then some you don't

want. __ Be care-ful what __ you wish for __ 'cause you just might get it all. __

__ You just might get it all, _____ yeah.

D.S. al Coda

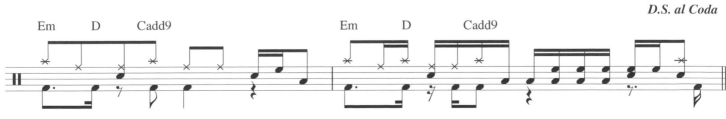

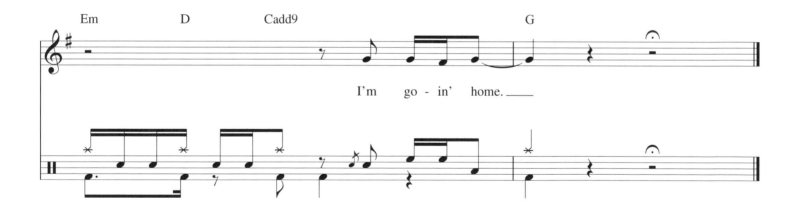

Additional Lyrics

2. The miles are getting longer, it seems,
   The closer I get to you.
   I've not always been the best man or friend for you,
   But your love remains true.
   And I don't know why
   You always seem to give me another try.

7 21 Guns

**Words and Music by David Bowie, John Phillips,
Billie Joe Armstrong, Mike Pritchard and Frank Wright**

Chorus

Verse

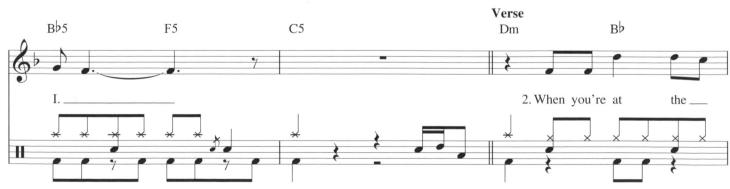

end of the road _ and you lost _ all sense of con-trol. _

And your thoughts _ have _ tak-en their toll _ when your mind _ breaks the spir-it of your

soul. _ Your faith _ walks on bro-ken glass _

and the hang-o-ver does-n't pass. _ Noth-ing's ev-er _

D.S. al Coda 1

built _ to last. _ You're in ru-ins. _

Verse

3. When it's time_ to _ live and let die _ and you can't get an - oth - er try, _

D.S. al Coda 2

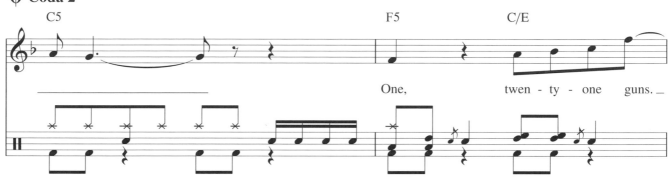

some-thing in - side this heart_ has died. _ You're in ru - ins.

Coda 2

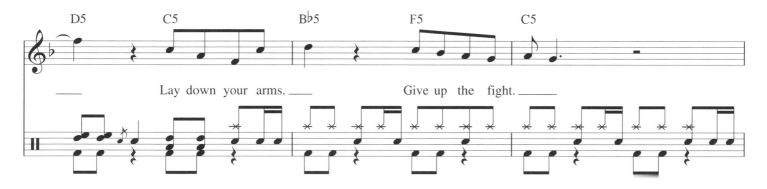

One, twen - ty - one guns. _

Lay down your arms. _ Give up the fight. _

One, twen - ty - one guns. _ Throw up your arms _ in - to the sky, _

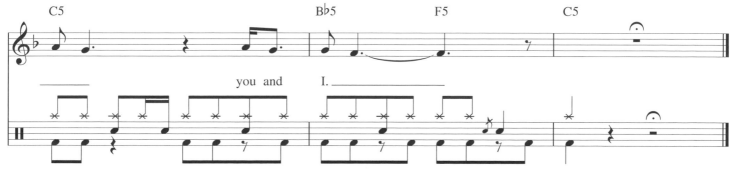

you and I. _

◆ 8 Use Somebody

Words and Music by Caleb Followill, Nathan Followill, Jared Followill and Matthew Followill

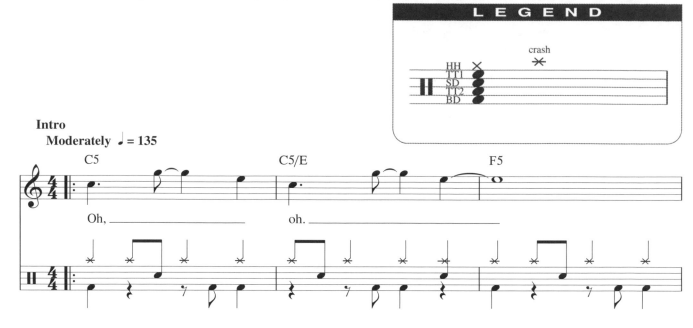

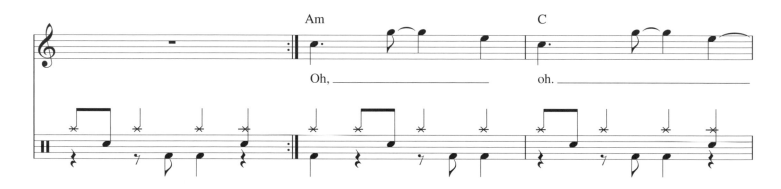

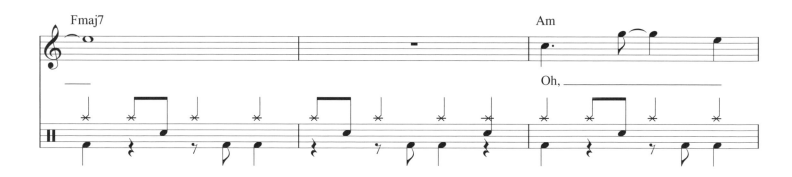

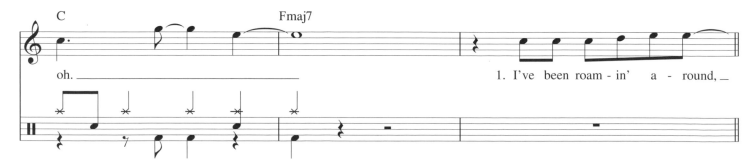

-er of ___ the street. ___ You know ___ that I could

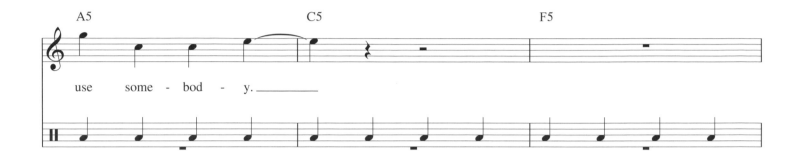

use some - bod - y. ___

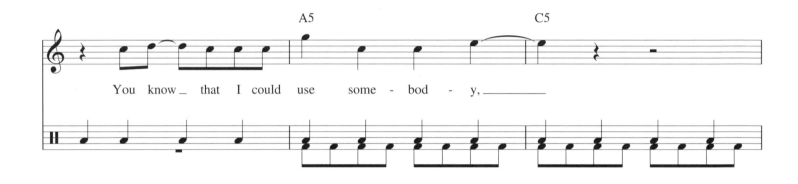

You know ___ that I could use some - bod - y, ___

𝄋 Chorus

some - one ___ like you. ___ 1., 2. Oh, ___

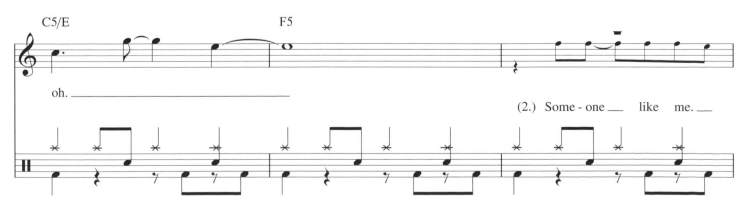

oh. ___

(2.) Some - one ___ like me. ___

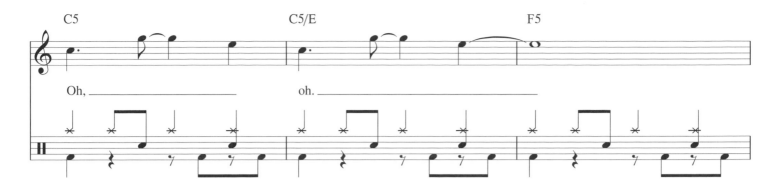

C5   C5/E   F5

Oh, _____ oh.

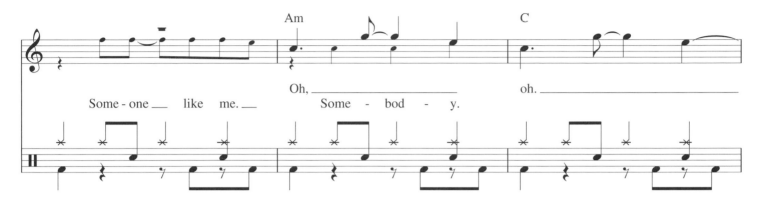

Am   C

Oh, _____ oh. _____

Some - one ___ like me. ___ Some - bod - y.

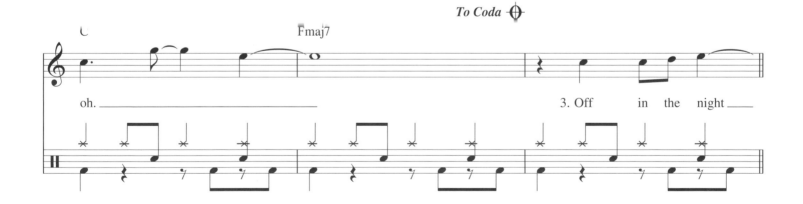

Fmaj7   Am

___ Oh, _____

To Coda ⊕

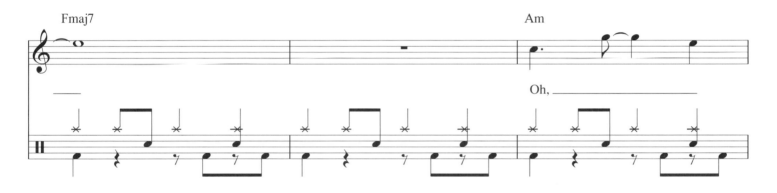

Fmaj7

oh. _____ 3. Off   in   the   night ___

Verse

N.C.(C5)   (C5/E)   (F5)

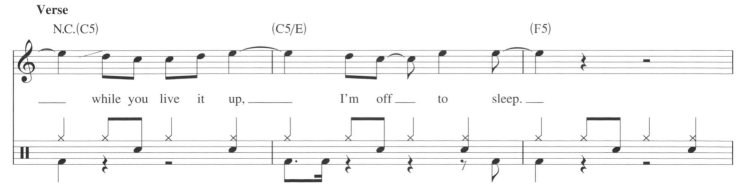

___ while you live it up, ___ I'm off ___ to sleep. ___

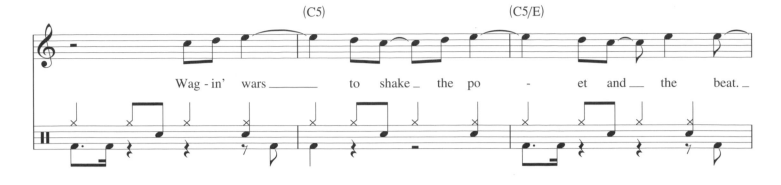

(C5)   (C5/E)

Wag - in' wars ___ to shake ___ the po - et and ___ the beat. ___

(F5)   A5

___   I hope ___ it's gon - na make you no - tice ___

C5   F5   A5

___   I hope ___ it's gon-na make you no - tice ___

D.S. al Coda

C5   F5

___   some - one ___ like me. ___

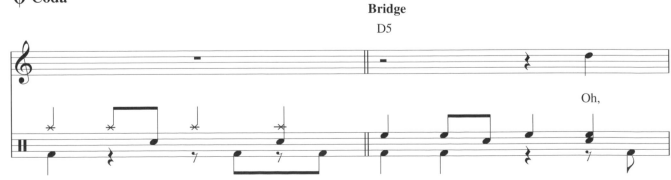

$\oplus$ **Coda**

Bridge

D5

Oh,

42

F#5

let it out. Oh, let it out. Oh, let it out. Oh,

D5   F#5

let it out. Oh, let it out. Oh, let it out. Oh,

Guitar Solo

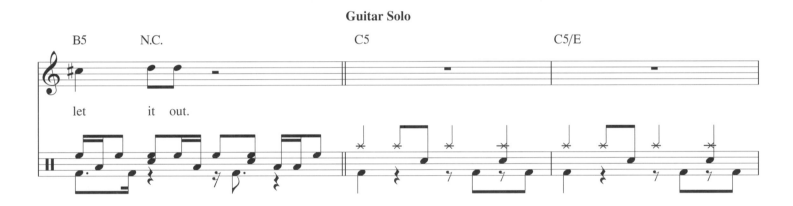

B5   N.C.   C5   C5/E

let it out.

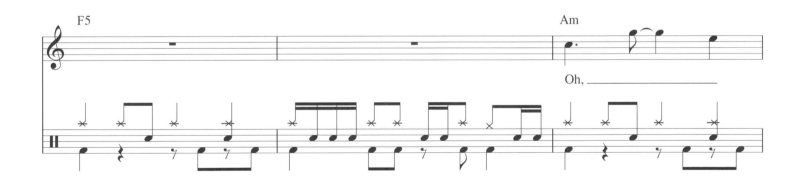

F5   Am

Oh, _____

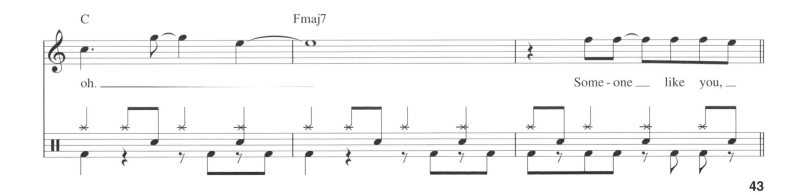

C   Fmaj7

oh. _____   Some - one __ like you, __

Chorus

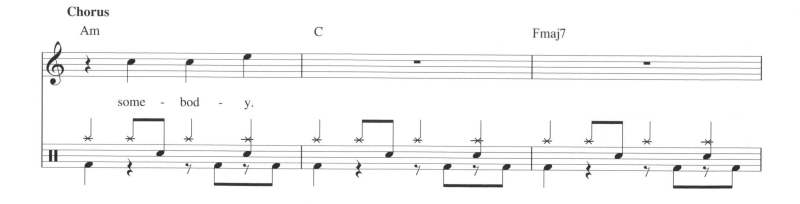

some - bod - y.

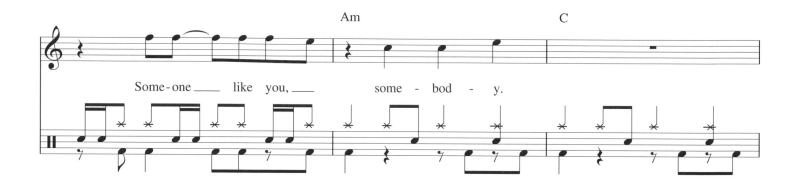

Some - one ___ like you, ___ some - bod - y.

Some - one ___ like you, ___ some - bod - y.

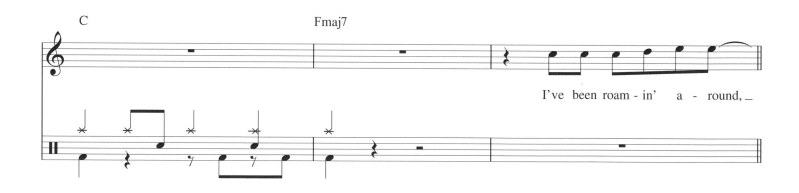

I've been roam - in' a - round, ___

Outro

Drums: don't play

C5   C5/E   F5

___ I was look - in' down ___ at all ___ I see. ___

FastTrack MUSIC INSTRUCTION

*Fast*Track is the fastest way for beginners to learn to play the instrument they just bought. *Fast*Track is different from other method books: we've made our book/CD packs user-friendly with plenty of cool songs that make it easy and fun for players to teach themselves. Plus, the last section of the *Fast*Track books have the same songs so that students can form a band and jam together. Songbooks for Guitar, Bass, Keyboard and Drums are all compatible, and feature eight songs including hits such as Wild Thing • Twist and Shout • Layla • Born to Be Wild • and more! All packs include a great play-along CD with a professional-sounding back-up band.

FASTTRACK GUITAR

For Electric or Acoustic Guitar – or both!
by Blake Neely & Jeff Schroedl
Book/CD Packs

Teaches music notation, tablature, full chords and power chords, riffs, licks, scales, and rock and blues styles. Method Book 1 includes 73 songs and examples.

LEVEL 1
00697282	Method Book – 9" x 12"	$7.99
00695390	Method Book – 5½" x 5"	$7.95
00697287	Songbook 1 – 9" x 12"	$12.95
00695397	Songbook 1 – 5½" x 5"	$9.95
00695343	Songbook 2	$12.95
00696438	Rock Songbook 1	$12.99
00696057	DVD	$7.99

LEVEL 2
00697280	Method Book	$9.99
00697296	Songbook 1	$12.95
00695344	Songbook 2	$12.95

CHORDS & SCALES
00697291	9" x 12"	$9.95
00696588	Spanish Edition	$9.99

FASTTRACK BASS

by Blake Neely & Jeff Schroedl
Book/CD Packs

Everything you need to know about playing the bass, including music notation, tablature, riffs, licks, scales, syncopation, and rock and blues styles. Method Book 1 includes 75 songs and examples.

LEVEL 1
00697284	Method Book – 9" x 12"	$7.95
00697289	Songbook 1 – 9" x 12"	$12.95
00695400	Songbook 1 – 5½" x 5"	$9.95
00695368	Songbook 2	$12.95
00696440	Rock Songbook 1	$12.99
00696058	DVD	$7.99

LEVEL 2
00697294	Method Book	$9.95
00697298	Songbook 1	$12.95
00695369	Songbook 2	$12.95

FASTTRACK KEYBOARD

For Electric Keyboard, Synthesizer, or Piano
by Blake Neely & Gary Meisner
Book/CD Packs

Learn how to play that piano today! With this book you'll learn music notation, chords, riffs, licks, scales, syncopation, and rock and blues styles. Method Book 1 includes over 87 songs and examples.

LEVEL 1
00697283	Method Book – 9" x 12"	$7.99
00697288	Songbook 1 – 9" x 12"	$12.95
00695366	Songbook 2	$12.95
00696439	Rock Songbook 1	$12.99
00696060	DVD	$7.99

LEVEL 2
00697293	Method Book	$9.95
00697297	Songbook 1	$12.95
00695370	Songbook 2	$12.99

CHORDS & SCALES
00697292	9" x 12"	$9.95

FASTTRACK DRUM

by Blake Neely & Rick Mattingly
Book/CD Packs

With this book, you'll learn music notation, riffs and licks, syncopation, rock, blues and funk styles, and improvisation. Method Book 1 includes over 75 songs and examples.

LEVEL 1
00697285	Method Book – 9" x 12"	$7.95
00695396	Method Book – 5½" x 5"	$7.95
00697290	Songbook 1 – 9" x 12"	$12.95
00695367	Songbook 2	$12.95
00696441	Rock Songbook 1	$12.99

LEVEL 2
00697295	Method Book	$9.95
00697299	Songbook 1	$12.95
00695371	Songbook 2	$12.95
00696059	DVD	$7.99

FASTTRACK SAXOPHONE

by Blake Neely
Book/CD Packs

With this book, you'll learn music notation; riffs, scales, keys; syncopation; rock and blues styles; and more. Includes 72 songs and examples.

LEVEL 1
00695241	Method Book	$7.95
00695409	Songbook	$12.95

FASTTRACK HARMONICA

by Blake Neely & Doug Downing
Book/CD Packs

These books cover all you need to learn C Diatonic harmonica, including: music notation • singles notes and chords • riffs, licks & scales • syncopation • rock and blues styles. Method Book 1 includes over 70 songs and examples.

LEVEL 1
00695407	Method Book	$7.99
00695574	Songbook	$12.95

LEVEL 2
00695889	Method Book	$9.95

FASTTRACK LEAD SINGER

by Blake Neely
Book/CD Packs

Everything you need to be a great singer, including: how to read music, microphone tips, warm-up exercises, ear training, syncopation, and more. Method Book 1 includes 80 songs and examples.

LEVEL 1
00695408	Method Book	$7.99
00695410	Songbook	$12.95
00696589	Spanish Edition	$7.99

LEVEL 2
00695892	Songbook 1	$12.95

FOR MORE INFORMATION, SEE YOUR LOCAL MUSIC DEALER, OR WRITE TO:

HAL•LEONARD®
CORPORATION

7777 W. BLUEMOUND RD. P.O. BOX 13819 MILWAUKEE, WI 53213

Prices, contents, and availability subject to change without notice. Some products may not be available outside the U.S.A.

Visit Hal Leonard online at **www.halleonard.com**

1211

HAL·LEONARD DRUM PLAY-ALONG

Play your favorite songs quickly and easily with the *Drum Play-Along*™ series. Just follow the drum notation, listen to the CD to hear how the drums should sound, then play along using the separate backing tracks. The lyrics are also included for quick reference. The audio CD is playable on any CD player. For PC and Mac computer users, the CD is enhanced so you can adjust the recording to any tempo without changing the pitch!

1. Pop/Rock
Hurts So Good • Message in a Bottle • No Reply at All • Owner of a Lonely Heart • Peg • Rosanna • Separate Ways (Worlds Apart) • Swingtown.
00699742 Book/CD Pack $12.95

2. Classic Rock
Barracuda • Come Together • Mississippi Queen • Radar Love • Space Truckin' • Walk This Way • White Room • Won't Get Fooled Again.
00699741 Book/CD Pack $12.95

3. Hard Rock
Bark at the Moon • Detroit Rock City • Living After Midnight • Panama • Rock You like a Hurricane • Run to the Hills • Smoke on the Water • War Pigs (Interpolating Luke's Wall).
00699743 Book/CD Pack $12.95

4. Modern Rock
Chop Suey! • Duality • Here to Stay • Judith • Nice to Know You • Nookie • One Step Closer • Whatever.
00699744 Book/CD Pack $12.95

5. Funk
Cissy Strut • Cold Sweat, Part 1 • Fight the Power, Part 1 • Flashlight • Pick Up the Pieces • Shining Star • Soul Vaccination • Superstition.
00699745 Book/CD Pack $12.95

6. '90s Rock
Alive • Been Caught Stealing • Cherub Rock • Give It Away • I'll Stick Around • Killing in the Name • Shine • Smells Like Teen Spirit.
00699746 Book/CD Pack $14.99

7. Punk Rock
All the Small Things • Brain Stew (The Godzilla Remix) • Buddy Holly • Dirty Little Secret • Fat Lip • Flavor of the Weak • Lifestyles of the Rich and Famous • Self Esteem.
00699747 Book/CD Pack $14.99

8. '80s Rock
Cult of Personality • Heaven's on Fire • Rock of Ages • Shake Me • Smokin' in the Boys Room • Talk Dirty to Me • We're Not Gonna Take It • You Give Love a Bad Name.
00699832 Book/CD Pack $12.95

9. Big Band
Christopher Columbus • Corner Pocket • Flying Home • In the Mood • Opus One • Stompin' at the Savoy • Take the "A" Train • Woodchopper's Ball.
00699833 Book/CD Pack $12.99

10. blink-182
Adam's Song • All the Small Things • Dammit • Feeling This • Man Overboard • The Rock Show • Stay Together for the Kids • What's My Age Again?
00699834 Book/CD Pack $14.95

11. Jimi Hendrix Experience: Smash Hits
All Along the Watchtower • Can You See Me? • Crosstown Traffic • Fire • Foxey Lady • Hey Joe • Manic Depression • Purple Haze • Red House • Remember • Stone Free • The Wind Cries Mary.
00699835 Book/CD Pack $16.95

12. The Police
Can't Stand Losing You • De Do Do Do, De Da Da Da • Don't Stand So Close to Me • Every Breath You Take • Every Little Thing She Does Is Magic • Spirits in the Material World • Synchronicity II • Walking on the Moon.
00700268 Book/CD Pack $14.99

13. Steely Dan
Deacon Blues • Do It Again • FM • Hey Nineteen • Josie • My Old School • Reeling in the Years.
00700202 Book/CD Pack $16.99

14. The Doors
Break on Through to the Other Side • Hello, I Love You (Won't You Tell Me Your Name?) • L.A. Woman • Light My Fire • Love Me Two Times • People Are Strange • Riders on the Storm • Roadhouse Blues.
00699887 Book/CD Pack $14.95

15. Lennon & McCartney
Back in the U.S.S.R. • Day Tripper • Drive My Car • Get Back • A Hard Day's Night • Paperback Writer • Revolution • Ticket to Ride.
00700271 Book/CD Pack $14.99

17. Nirvana
About a Girl • All Apologies • Come As You Are • Dumb • Heart Shaped Box • In Bloom • Lithium • Smells like Teen Spirit.
00700273 Book/CD Pack $14.95

18. Motown
Ain't Too Proud to Beg • Dancing in the Street • Get Ready • How Sweet It Is (To Be Loved by You) • I Can't Help Myself (Sugar Pie, Honey Bunch) • Sir Duke • Stop! in the Name of Love • You've Really Got a Hold on Me.
00700274 Book/CD Pack $12.99

19. Rock Band: Modern Rock Edition
Are You Gonna Be My Girl • Black Hole Sun • Creep • Dani California • In Bloom • Learn to Fly • Say It Ain't So • When You Were Young.
00700707 Book/CD Pack $14.95

20. Rock Band: Classic Rock Edition
Ballroom Blitz • Detroit Rock City • Don't Fear the Reaper • Gimme Shelter • Highway Star • Mississippi Queen • Suffragette City • Train Kept A-Rollin'.
00700708 Book/CD Pack $14.95

21. Weezer
Beverly Hills • Buddy Holly • Dope Nose • Hash Pipe • My Name Is Jonas • Pork and Beans • Say It Ain't So • Undone – The Sweater Song.
00700959 Book/CD Pack $14.99

24. Pink Floyd – Dark Side of the Moon
Any Colour You Like • Brain Damage • Breathe • Eclipse • Money • Time • Us and Them.
00701612 Book/CD Pack $14.99

27. Modern Worship
Beautiful One • Days of Elijah • Hear Our Praises • Holy Is the Lord • How Great Is Our God • I Give You My Heart • Worthy Is the Lamb • You Are Holy (Prince of Peace).
00701921 Book/CD Pack $12.99

FOR MORE INFORMATION, SEE YOUR LOCAL MUSIC DEALER, OR WRITE TO:

HAL·LEONARD® CORPORATION
7777 W. BLUEMOUND RD. P.O. BOX 13819
MILWAUKEE, WISCONSIN 53213

Prices, contents and availability subject to change without notice and may vary outside the US.

Visit Hal Leonard Online at
www.halleonard.com

0511

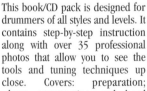